world tour
Australia

LEIGH ANN COBB

www.raintreepublishers.co.uk

Visit our website to find out more information about Raintree books.

To order:
- ☎ Phone 44 (0) 1865 888112
- 📄 Send a fax to 44 (0) 1865 314091
- 💻 Visit the Raintree Bookshop at **www.raintreepublishers.co.uk** to browse our catalogue and order online.

First published in Great Britain by Raintree Publishers, Halley Court, Jordan Hill, Oxford, OX2 8EJ, part of Harcourt Education.
Raintree is a registered trademark of Harcourt Education Ltd.

© Harcourt Education Ltd 2003
First published in paperback 2004
The moral right of the proprieter has been asserted.

Editorial: Sally Knowles
Cover Design: Peter Bailey and Michelle Lisseter
Production: Jonathan Smith

Printed and bound in China and Hong Kong by South China Printing Company

ISBN 1 844 21310 2 (hardback)
07 06 05 04 03
10 9 8 7 6 5 4 3 2 1

ISBN 1 844 21324 2 (paperback)
08 07 06 05 04
10 9 8 7 6 5 4 3 2 1

British Library Cataloguing in Publication Data
Cobb, Leigh Anne
Australia (World tour)
994
A full catalogue for this book is available from the British Library

Acknowledgements
The publishers would like to thank the following for permission to reproduce photographs: p.**5** ©M. Harvey/DRK Photo; p.**7** ©Charles Lenars/CORBIS; p.**8** ©Bob & Suzanne Clemenz; p.**15b** ©Joe McDonald/CORBIS; p.**19** ©Ron Dorman/Superstock; p.**21b** ©Jeffry L. Rotman/AGPix; p.**23** ©Bill Bachman; p.**24a** ©Don Pitcher; p.**24b** ©John W. Banagan/Getty Images; p.**27b** ©Siegfried Tauquer/eStock Photo; p.**28** ©Penny Tweedie/CORBIS; p.**29** ©Don Pitcher; p.**31a** ©Bill Bachman; p.**33** ©Paul Chesley/Getty Images; p.**34** ©Michael Freeman/CORBIS; p.**35** ©Foodpix; p.**37a** ©Victoria Dock/Trip/Eric Smith; p.**37b** ©Peter Mead/Tom Stack & Associates; p.**40** ©Trip/Eric Smith; p.**42** ©Ron Dorman/Superstock; p. **44a** ©CORBIS; p.**44b** ©Rufus F. Folkks/CORBIS; p.**44c** ©Jerry Lampen/CORBIS.

Additional Photography by Corbis Royalty Free, Comstock Royalty Free, Getty Images Royalty Free PhotoDisc, and the Steck-Vaughn Collection.

Cover photography: Background: Getty Images/Taxi/Terry Qing. Foreground: Getty Images/Stone/Paul Chesley

Contents

Welcome to Australia

When visitors fly into Australia, most of the country looks like one huge desert. There is a lot more than desert in Australia, from big cities to fascinating wildlife like koalas and kangaroos. If you are curious to find out more about this fascinating country, you are sure to find something to interest you.

Reader's tips:

• Look at the pictures

This book has lots of great photos. Flip through and look at the pictures you like best. This is a good way to get a quick idea of what this book is all about.

• Read the captions

When you come to a picture that interests you, read the caption next to it. The captions will tell you all about what you are looking at. Then read the text to learn more.

• Use the index

If you are looking for a certain fact, you might want to turn to the index at the back of the book. The index lists the subjects covered in the book. It will tell you what pages to find them on.

▲ UNDERWATER ADVENTURES

On your Australian adventure, be sure to go snorkelling on the Great Barrier Reef. You will see fish that do not live anywhere else in the world. You can visit more than 600 little islands off Australia's eastern coast.

Australia's past

Australia has a colourful history. It is one of the oldest land masses on the Earth but life here is always changing.

Ancient history

The first people to live in Australia were the Aborigines who came from Asia between 120,000 and 60,000 years ago. The Aborigines were great hunters and wandered the **continent**, using the land and its **natural resources** with great care. They believed that people could not own land and felt they belonged to the land.

European settlement

Dutchman Willem Jansz was the first European to land in Australia. He explored the eastern coast of the Gulf of Carpentaria. Other explorers from Europe followed, but at first Europeans were not interested in Australia because it looked too dry to grow crops.

In 1770, Captain James Cook, a navigator in the British navy, landed at Botany Bay on Australia's **fertile** eastern coast. There, Captain Cook discovered some of Australia's **unique** plants and animals. The Botany Bay area later became the city of Sydney.

At the time of Captain Cook's voyage, Great Britain was having problems. British jails were becoming too crowded and there was nowhere to put the criminals. The British also needed raw materials, such as wood from trees, to build ships and to supply other industries.

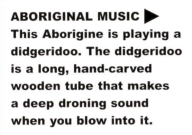

ABORIGINAL MUSIC ▶
This Aborigine is playing a
didgeridoo. The didgeridoo
is a long, hand-carved
wooden tube that makes
a deep droning sound
when you blow into it.

The British decided that Australia was the answer to
these problems. It was the perfect place to send
criminals, who would serve their sentences doing work
for their country. The **convicts** would grow crops, dig
mines for valuable metals and look for other useful raw
materials needed by Great Britain.

Australia became a **penal colony**. Captain Arthur
Phillip led the first British fleet there. He took eleven
ships with 736 convicts and more than 250 free people
into Sydney Harbour in 1788. Over time, a total of
160,000 convicts were taken to Australia. They faced
many hardships. Most had not done this kind of work
before. Supplies took months to arrive from their
homeland and barely lasted until the next ship arrived.

▲ **SHOPPING ON THE ROCKS**
Called 'The Rocks' after the rocky shoreline nearby, this famous area of Sydney is where the first Europeans came to Australia. Today it is a charming shopping district and a great place for finding souvenirs to bring home.

Riches unfold

Gradually, other settlers began to explore Australia and find places to live. They moved inland from the Sydney area in all directions. Brisbane, Perth, Melbourne and Adelaide were some of the first cities.

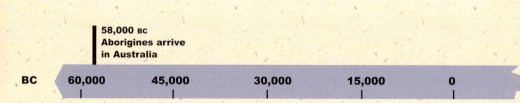

58,000 BC
Aborigines arrive
in Australia

BC   60,000   45,000   30,000   15,000   0

Land suitable for grazing animals was discovered. John MacArthur, a wealthy landowner, was the first to import sheep from Spain. He started Australia's great wool industry, which still flourishes today.

Eventually, the bravest explorers made their way to the huge deserts of the Australian Outback. Many turned back but when gold was discovered in the 1850s, **immigrants** came from Europe, China and America hoping to make their fortunes.

As more land was settled, the cities grew, pushing the Aborigines out of their tribal lands. Australia was declared a nation on 1 January 1901.

Australia today

Australia still has connections with Great Britain. Some Australians want it to become an independent republic, rather than remaining part of the **commonwealth** of Great Britain. Many Asian people have moved to Australia. In fact, Asians make up the largest minority group in the nation. Australia has helped many **refugees** when their homelands were in crisis.

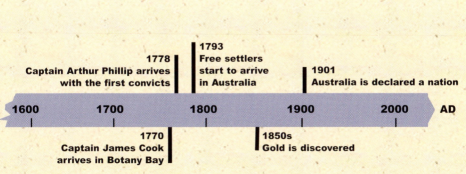

1778
Captain Arthur Phillip arrives with the first convicts

1793
Free settlers start to arrive in Australia

1901
Australia is declared a nation

1600   1700   1800   1900   2000   AD

1770
Captain James Cook arrives in Botany Bay

1850s
Gold is discovered

A look at Australia's geography

Land

Australia is the flattest of all the continents. The highest point is Mount Kosciusko at 2228 metres. The lowest point is Lake Eyre at 16 metres below **sea level**. Australia is also the driest continent. The coastal areas are very different to the interior and are fertile and hilly. Rainforests can be found in the north. Most Australians live along the eastern coast.

The Great Dividing Range is a system of mountain ranges that separates the eastern coastal area from the Central Lowlands. The inland region is known as the Outback. It consists of dusty plains with low bushes and stark gum trees and is a breathtaking sight. Surprisingly, people do live in some parts of this desert-like place. There are a few mountains in the Outback, such as the Macdonnell Ranges near Alice Springs, and the occasional salt lake. The Great **Artesian Basin** runs under the Central Lowlands. Ranchers of the Outback use this water source to **irrigate** the land for grazing livestock.

The Great Western Plateau covers most of the states of Western Australia, the Northern Territory and South Australia. The plateau is higher than the Central Lowlands and is very flat. Crops and livestock are raised where rainfall is heaviest – in the north and south-west.

AUSTRALIA'S SIZE ▶
Australia covers
about 7.5 million
sq km (3 million
sq miles). It is
3940 km (2450 miles)
long from north to
south and 4350 km
(2700 miles) wide
from east to west.

ASIA

PACIFIC
OCEAN

INDIAN
OCEAN

N
W   E
S

INDONESIA

PAPUA NEW
GUINEA

Arafura Sea

Timor
Sea

•Darwin

Coral
Sea

INDIAN
OCEAN

Alice Springs •

A U S T R A L I A

Brisbane •

•Perth

Adelaide•

Canberra
★

• Sydney

Melbourne •

Tasman
Sea

Tasmania

•Hobart

AUSTRALIA

★   National capital

•   Major city

—   River

0   300   600 Kilometres
0   300   600 Miles

Water

Australia is separated from Asia by the Timor Sea and the Arafura Sea. The Coral Sea Islands to the north border the Great Barrier Reef. The Tasman Sea separates Australia from New Zealand in the south-east and the Indian Ocean lies between Australia and Antarctica to the south.

The only permanently flowing rivers in Australia are found in the eastern and south-western parts of the country and on the island of Tasmania. The longest river, the Darling, starts in the north-eastern state of Queensland. The river Murray starts from the Mount Kosciusko area and is fed by melting snow. All other rivers are seasonal or temporary in their flow. They have water in some seasons and are dry riverbeds in others.

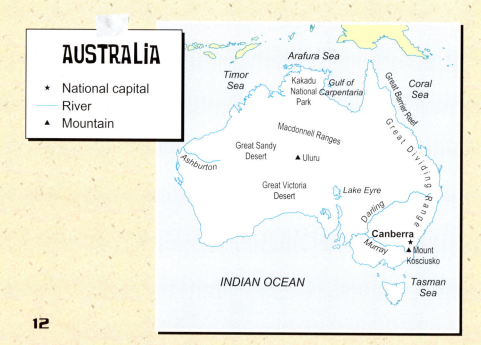

AUSTRALIA

- ★ National capital
- — River
- ▲ Mountain

Arafura Sea

Timor Sea

Kakadu National Park

Gulf of Carpentaria

Great Barrier Reef

Coral Sea

Macdonnell Ranges

Great Sandy Desert

▲ Uluru

Great Victoria Desert

Lake Eyre

Ashburton

Darling

Great Dividing Range

Canberra ★

Murray

▲ Mount Kosciusko

INDIAN OCEAN

Tasman Sea

▲ **THE TWELVE APOSTLES**
As one huge island, Australia has a long coastline.
Spectacular rock formations like the Twelve Apostles,
seen here, invite visitors to explore the shore.

Weather

Australians celebrate New Year during their summer. Australia is in the southern hemisphere, below the **equator**, on the bottom half of the globe. Europe and the USA are in the northern hemisphere, on the top half of the globe. Australia's seasons are the opposite to Europe's. When it is winter in Europe, it is summer in Australia. Australians enjoy autumn while it is springtime in Europe.

For most of the year, Australia is dry and hot. However, in the winter, there is skiing in Tasmania or on Mount Kosciusko. You can also enjoy scuba diving on the Great Barrier Reef.

In the summer, temperatures in some places can soar above 38°C. The Outback gets only about 500 millimetres of rainfall per year. That is not enough rain for many plants to grow. The **temperate** southern and eastern regions and tropical northern regions get enough rain to support lots of plant life.

CUDDLY KOALAS ▶
Koalas grow to about 9 kilograms, which is slightly larger than a domestic cat. They are found only in the forests of Australia and eat the leaves of eucalyptus trees.

▲ **IT'S A HARD LIFE**
This red kangaroo is taking a break in the dry heat of the Outback's open plains. It is a good thing that kangaroos need very little water to survive.

Sydney: snapshot of a big city

▲ SYDNEY – SOARING SONGS AND SKYSCRAPERS
Be sure to visit the world-famous Sydney Opera House, which stands out in Sydney Harbour in front of the skyscrapers. Performers come here from all over the world.

Sydney is a fascinating city where there is always plenty happening. Skyscrapers stand alongside historic buildings. There are restaurants serving food from all over the world and beautiful beaches and a breathtaking waterfront to explore.

City facts

Sydney is Australia's oldest and largest city, but it is not the capital – Canberra is. More than 4 million people live in Sydney – over 20 per cent of Australia's total population. Sydney is considered to be the economic and cultural centre of Australia.

Sydney lies on the south-eastern shore of Australia, off the Tasman Sea. It used to be the home of the Daruk Aborigines. The city was first settled at Circular Quay, originally Sydney Cove. Today it spreads out from here and there are 750 **suburbs**.

A buzzing metropolis

Sydney is one of the nicest cities in the world. It has a central business district with huge skyscrapers, and the beautiful waterfront and **wharf** of Sydney Harbour.

The people of Sydney are known for their friendliness. More than 100,000 international visitors to the 2000 Olympic Games experienced this. The city hosted a big party for its guests. Australians cheered on other teams to victory as well as their own.

Getting away from it all

Sydney's harbour is the focal point of the city. It serves as both playground and major port, busy with ferries and yachts. To the north and south of the city are white sandy beaches and dramatic cliff scenery, only minutes away from the city centre by car or ferry. Taking a harbour walk is a lovely way to get to know Sydney Harbour and its position on the ocean.

One spectacular walk starts at The Gap, an ocean cliff at Watson's Bay. This walk includes breathtaking views of the city, the harbour channels and some of the world's finest beaches.

There is no better place to get a taste of Australian beach culture than at Bondi Beach. It is in east Sydney and is easy to get to by public transport. This world-famous beach is perfect for year-round surfing, playing beach games like volleyball, flying a kite or strolling along the promenade.

SYDNEY BY ROAD ▶
Motorways reach across Sydney to bring in tourists and residents. If you are travelling by car, head downtown for shopping and then straight to Bondi Beach for fun in the sun.

SYDNEY'S TOP-TEN CHECKLIST

Here is a list of the ten things you should try to do if you go to Sydney.

☐ Visit Sydney Opera House and see an opera, ballet or play.

☐ Climb the arches of the Sydney Harbour Bridge.

☐ Go up to the observation level of the AMP Centrepoint Tower for a view of the whole city.

☐ Visit the site of the first colonial settlement in 1788.

☐ Wander The Rocks historic district for people-watching and interesting shops..

☐ Swim in the pool at the Aquatic Centre.

☐ Go on a harbour cruise to Manly Wharf and visit the aquarium called Oceanworld.

☐ Learn about Aborigine culture from cave art at Botany Bay National Park.

☐ Browse through the Harbourside Shopping Complex's 200 stores.

☐ Try the best of international cuisine in Darlinghurst or Kings Cross.

Four top sights

The Great Barrier Reef

The Great Barrier Reef is off the coast of Queensland. It extends along Australia's north-east coast for more than 2000 kilometres (1250 miles) and covers 350,000 square kilometres (135,000 square miles). There is diving all year round along its coral reef. The reef is the longest in the world and includes 700 islands.

There are 350 different kinds of coral. Coral reefs are made up of hardened skeletons of dead sea animals and coral polyps. If you dive, you may wonder why the coral does not look as colourful as it does on videos. The colour is there; you just need white light, as used on a video camera, to shine on it so it will reflect its natural colour. This is why night diving is spectacular.

There are many colourful animals that live along the reef. There are 1500 **species** of fish, sixteen species of sea snake and six species of sea turtle. Some divers wonder if they will see a shark while diving. This is not likely, but if they do, it will probably be a white-tip reef shark or a black-tip reef shark. Luckily, like most sharks, they like to eat fish best. They are shy and stay away from people. But watch out for Great White sharks too.

If you prefer, you can explore sea life without getting wet. Reef HQ, in nearby Townsville, is the largest living coral-reef aquarium in the world.

▼ NO PLACE FOR A STROLL

Scratchy, rock-hard coral makes up the Great Barrier Reef. It is home to so many species of sea life that you will run out of snorkelling time before you can see them all.

SHARK ALERT! ▶

Great white sharks like this one enjoy the warm waters of the Great Barrier Reef. A steel cage protects these divers while they study the sharks.

Uluru (Ayers Rock)

Uluru is in the Australian Outback in Australia's Northern Territory. It stands 348 metres tall and is 3.5 kilometres (2.2 miles) long. It used to be called Ayers Rock but the Aboriginal name is used now. Uluru is a sacred site to the Aborigines and they prefer that people do not climb the rock. Instead, walk along the marked paths found around the rock.

Walking around the base of Uluru is exciting. There are small caves that have walls covered with paintings made by Aborigines many years ago. Most of the rock art tells stories from Dreamtime. In Aboriginal stories, Dreamtime is the time when god-like beings created the land. One story says the Red Lizard Tatji's stick got stuck in the rock. His efforts to dig the stick out led to the bowl-shaped caves.

Uluru is actually grey, but it has a coating of iron oxide. This **mineral** coating gives it a red and pink tint. The colour of the rock appears to change as the sun shines on it at different times of day.

FASCINATING FACT

The Aborigines invented the boomerang, a piece of hardwood carved into a simple V-shaped curve. It travels away from its thrower before changing direction and coming back towards the thrower. This happens because of the way air acts on its curves.

▲ **ABORIGINE SPEAR-THROWING**
On a tour of Uluru, you can learn how to throw a spear like the Aborigines do. This tour guide is demonstrating how to throw a spear called a mira.

◀ **AT THE BEACH**
These surfers are up for fun and adventure. Surfing is very popular in Australia, so be sure to catch a wave. There are classes for beginners.

▲ **ONE THOUSAND SHADES OF GREEN**
Melbourne's Botanical Gardens are a popular place with locals and tourists. Have a picnic by the lake, a pretty spot to sit and plan the rest of your day.

24

Melbourne

Melbourne, on the southern coast, is the youngest city of its size in the world. A group of businessmen bought the land from the Aborigines in 1835. Soon, another group set up camp across the Yarra River from these first settlers.

Melbourne was declared a city in 1847 and then grew as a result of the Gold Rush. Melbourne was the temporary capital of Australia while Canberra was being built. Many people from Europe, Vietnam and Cambodia have moved to Melbourne.

Visitors to Melbourne can enjoy the beauty of its buildings and the varied wildlife in its many public parks and gardens.

A stroll through Healesville Sanctuary may bring you face to face with a duck-billed platypus. A platypus is a shy, furry animal with a bill like a duck and a body like a beaver. It lives in fresh water. It is a mammal, which means that it is warm-blooded and produces milk to feed its babies. However, unlike other mammals, it lays eggs rather than giving birth to live babies. This special animal can only be found in Australia and Tasmania.

There are some very good places to go shopping on the Southbank between the Yarra River and the Victoria Arts Centre. Enjoy an exotic fruit from Queen Victoria Market or walk around the colourful and trendy Fitzroy district, a great place to people-watch.

Kakadu National Park

Many of the tourists who come to Australia want to see as much of the unique wildlife as possible. There is no better place to do this than Kakadu National Park in the Northern Territory – a true marvel of Australia. The best time to visit is in July and August, known as 'the Dry', when the wildlife is easier to find.

Take a cruise on South Alligator River or Yellow Water **Billabong**. Look for the tell-tale swirl near the water surface that the silver barramundi (a type of fish) creates. You can find this big fish only in Australia.

There are nature walks led by park rangers who talk about the history and wildlife of Kakadu National Park. Some animals are found only in this park. Among the 60 different mammals that live there are 26 species of bat.

While exploring Kakadu, you must see the animal that Australia is most famous for – the kangaroo. In Kakadu, you can see mobs of kangaroos at dawn or dusk. The antilopine wallaroo is the largest kangaroo of Northern Australia. Look for the reddish-coloured males and bluish-grey females and young.

Kangaroos are marsupials. That means that they give birth to babies that are not fully developed. The babies continue their growth inside a pouch in their mothers' bodies. A baby kangaroo is called a joey.

BIRD WATCHING ▶
You will see colourful little birds like these in Kakadu National Park, home to about 275 species of bird.

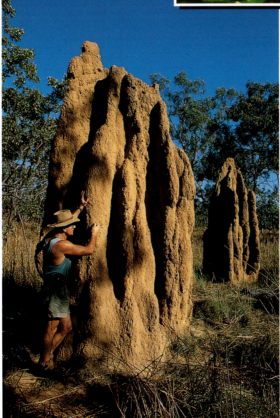

◀ **HIKING IN A WORLD OF WONDERS**
Kakadu National Park is also home to over 7000 sites of Aboriginal rock art. There are ten settlements where many Aborigines live and work to maintain the park.

Going to school in Australia

In Australia, children attend school from the age of five until they are sixteen. Then they can either leave or continue until they are seventeen or eighteen. Students usually choose to continue to the final year which qualifies them to enter a college or university.

Education is available to every child in Australia, as the responsibility of the state governments. Even children who live in the Outback, far from any school, are not excluded. They receive their lessons over the radio or on the computer and can post or e-mail their work.

▲ AN AUSTRALIAN CLASSROOM
This girl is working hard to make the grade.

Australian sports

Australians make great use of their pleasant climate and beaches by playing all kinds of different sports, including cricket, tennis, rugby and football. Look for the green-and-gold colours of the Australian kit when you watch international sport.

Most children learn how to swim because there are so many beaches and pools in Australia.

Horse racing is also very popular. There is a national holiday on the day the famous Melbourne Cup horse race takes place, even though the race lasts only a few minutes. It is held on the first Tuesday in November.

▲ SURFING
Surfers come from all over the world to catch a wave at one of Australia's many beautiful beaches.

From farming to factories

Agriculture, or farming, is an important business in Australia. The country leads the world in wool production. About 14 per cent of all the sheep in the world live in Australia. In addition to raising sheep, Australian farmers grow grapes for wine-making, cereals, fruit, dairy produce, meat and sugar cane.

Mining is very important to Australia, which is rich in mineral resources. Iron ore, nickel, diamonds, gold and natural gas come from western Australia. Queensland is rich in black coal, lead, zinc and silver. New South Wales and Victoria produce metals, as well as off-shore oil. Forestry is another important industry. Farmers grow trees and cut them down for wood. Then they replant the forests to grow more trees. Fishing is also important. Most of the fishing in Australia is for crustaceans – sea animals with a hard outer shell, such as crabs and lobsters. Also, many Australians work for the car industry, designing, building and selling cars.

The largest and fastest-growing businesses provide people with services they need. These services are things like telephone lines, e-mail and hotels. Tourism brings in lots of money and creates jobs for people who work in hotels, drive taxis or run museums.

Australians work in almost every other job that you can think of. Some are doctors or teachers. Some are writers or actors. All of them buy and sell things using the Australian dollar. The Australian dollar is the currency used in Australia.

OUTBACK OASES ▶
These welcome service areas are popping up in the once-empty Outback. You can fill up with fuel and then get a bite to eat at the cafe next door.

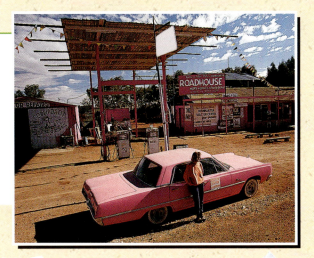

▼ **SHEEP-FARMER AT WORK**
Sheep are found in many parts of Australia, which produces more wool than any other country in the world. This sheep-farmer is rounding up her sheep to return to the farm.

The Australian government

Australia is a constitutional monarchy. The monarch (king or queen) of the United Kingdom is also head of state in Australia. A governor-general represents this monarch in Australia, but the governor-general has no real power. The power is held by the Australian parliament, led by the Australian prime minister.

Australia's government is a **federation**. The power is divided between the federal government and the state governments.

Australia is divided into six states and two territories: Australian Capital Territory, New South Wales, Northern Territory, Queensland, South Australia, Tasmania, Victoria and Western Australia.

AUSTRALIA'S NATIONAL FLAG

The flag is made up of three parts: the Union flag in the top left corner, the Star of Federation in the bottom left corner and the Southern Cross on the right half of the flag. The Union flag represents the British as the first Europeans to settle in Australia.

The Star of Federation has seven points. Six stand for the six Australian states. The seventh represents Australia's territories. The Southern Cross is an arrangement of stars that is visible in the night sky from anywhere in Australia.

Religions of Australia

People in Australia practise many different religions. Most of the original European settlers were Christians. Since then, immigrants from all over the world have brought other faiths including Islam, Buddhism and Judaism to Australia.

Many Aborigines practise their own religion, which centres around belief in the Dreamtime. This was the period when they believe beings with super powers, like gods, goddesses and magical animals, created the universe. Aborigines are organized into tribes and **clans**. The stories of Dreamtime are handed down through each generation by storytelling and colourful **symbolic** dancing.

ANCIENT TRADITION ▶
This young Aborigine and his relatives are preparing to take part in a traditional dance ceremony. Such ceremonies keep Aborigine traditions alive for the next generations.

Australian food

Australia is a huge country with a lot of delicious foods to try. Since the ocean surrounds Australia, there is always the freshest seafood available. Another Australian speciality is tropical fruit, like kiwi fruits, apricots, lychees and custard apples.

Beef, lamb and dairy products are plentiful in the grocery stores and restaurants. There are also lots of local meats such as kangaroo, buffalo, crocodile and emu.

Barbecues, or 'barbies', are a favourite Australian tradition. When the weather is nice, families gather to grill steaks, burgers, shrimps and other foods. They talk, eat and enjoy spending time outdoors. Be sure to include a 'barbie' on your trip to Australia.

▲ **AN ADVENTURE IN FOOD**
This is crocodile soup. This unusual dish can be sampled on crocodile farms in Australia.

Australia's recipe

STRAWBERRY PAVLOVA

INGREDIENTS:

3 egg whites
$\frac{1}{2}$ tsp vanilla
1 tsp cream of tartar
175 g sugar
125 g sliced strawberries
300 ml double cream

WARNING:

Never cook or bake by yourself. Always ask an adult to help you in the kitchen.

DIRECTIONS:

Whisk the egg whites in a bowl until they are stiff. Add the sugar gradually, whisking all the time, until the mixture forms soft peaks. Add the cream of tartar and vanilla essence. Meanwhile, draw a circle with diameter 25 cm on a piece of baking paper and place it on a baking sheet.

Add the sugar, 1 tablespoon at a time, beating quickly until very stiff peaks form and the sugar is almost dissolved (about 5 minutes).

Using the back of a spoon, spread the meringue on to the baking paper, building the sides up to form a bowl shape. Bake at 150°C (gas mark 2) for 35 minutes. Turn off the oven and let the meringue dry in the oven with the door closed for one hour. Remove the meringue from the baking sheet and pull off the baking paper.

FILLINGS

The traditional filling is fresh fruit and whipped cream. Whip the cream and use it to fill the bowl-shaped meringue. Place the fruit on top and serve.

Up close: Tasmania and its devils

Tasmania is Australia's smallest state and it is made up of several islands. The heart-shaped main island of Tasmania is the largest. It is about 320 kilometres (200 miles) wide and long. In the middle of the island are mountains and there are beautiful beaches around the coast.

The Aborigines once lived in Tasmania, but their population became much smaller after the arrival of the Europeans. The first European to discover the islands was the Dutch explorer Abel Tasman and Tasmania was named after him. Soon after, the British arrived. They developed shipbuilding and service industries.

Tasmania is secluded and separate from the rest of Australia. It has very special and rare wildlife that is not found elsewhere. Perhaps the most famous animal is the Tasmanian devil.

The Tasmanian devil is the largest meat-eating marsupial. As a marsupial, it carries its babies in a pouch until they are ready to come out – just like a kangaroo. The devil is only the size of a small dog. It earned a bad reputation from the first Europeans to see it. They heard its spine-chilling screeches and watched it fiercely tear into its **prey**, eating everything including bones and fur. It has very powerful jaws and teeth that are almost as strong as a crocodile's.

Tasmanian devils are scavengers, eating anything that is available, mainly dead animals but they will also attack a wounded or young animal. They can eat almost half their body weight in only 30 minutes.

WATERFALLS OF TASMANIA ▶

The Tasmanian islands have beautiful waterfalls. Some people say that once you go there, you will never want to leave.

▼ HOBART WATERFRONT

Shipbuilding was a very big industry at one time. Today, the harbour in the city of Hobart is a quiet and welcoming place to spend the afternoon.

37

▲ A DEVIL OF A NOISE
The screeches of this little Tasmanian devil warn other animals not to come too close.

WILD DOG ▶
Dingoes are wild dogs. They are very playful when left alone, but they cause problems too. They can upset the natural balance of animals in a region. You can find dingoes in parks and reserves throughout Australia.

Most sightings of Tasmanian devils occur when they are feeding and are showing threatening behaviour towards each other. But if you watch carefully you will discover that it is a shy animal, mostly keeping to itself. It is very tender and caring with its young. Tasmanian devils may make a lot of scary noises, but they can be very gentle with each other, too.

The population of devils in Tasmania can reach 150,000, especially following their mating season in March. Devils must compete for everything they need for survival – food, shelter and finding a mate.

The devils once lived on the mainland of Australia, but they disappeared with the arrival of the dingoes that were introduced by the Aborigines. The dingo is a type of wild dog.

Dingoes are introduced animals. That means they are not originally from Australia and were brought from elsewhere. In the natural environment, things must be kept in balance in order for everything to be able to survive. That includes plants, animals and water. Dingoes have upset that balance by killing and eating too many of certain animals. Dingoes threaten the survival of animals like the Tasmanian devil and the sea turtle. Many people are now working to help these and other endangered animals survive.

Holidays

Australians celebrate many national and religious holidays. Australia Day is 26 January. On this day in 1788, Captain Arthur Phillip arrived at Botany Bay at Sydney Cove, claiming the land for Great Britain. Some of the local holiday activities include banquets, marathons, rowing competitions and lively parades.

Anzac Day on the 25 April remembers those who have died serving their country. It is named after the Australia and New Zealand Army Corps in the First World War. Anzac Day usually begins with the Dawn Service. Military men and women all over Australia march to their local war memorials. Many Australians also celebrate the Christian festivals of Good Friday, Easter Monday and Christmas. There are also individual public holidays marked by each state.

◀ **ANZAC DAY**
These proud military men and women are marching in honour of Australia's and New Zealand's war heroes.

Learning the language

The national language of Australia is English. Some words in Australian slang English are different to those in other countries.

English	Australian	How to say it
Hello	G'day	G-DAY
Goodbye	Hooroo	HOO-roo
I think	I reckon	EYE RECK-in
Woman	Sheila	SHEE-lah
Man	Bloke	BLOKE

Quick facts

Australia

Capital
Canberra

Borders
Lies between the
Pacific and the
Indian Oceans
Nearest neighbour is
Papua New Guinea (NE)

Area
7,686,850 sq km
(2,967,897 sq miles)

Population
19,773,000

▼ **Largest cities**
Sydney (4,194,900 people)
Melbourne (3,562,200)
Brisbane (1,538,000)
Perth (1,356,000)
Adelaide (1,081,000)

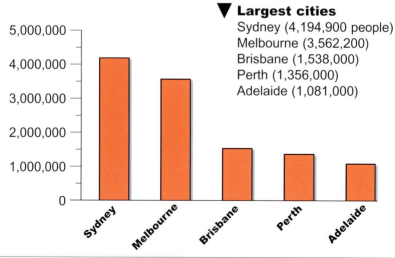

▲ Flag of Australia

Longest river
Murray
2589 km (1609 miles)

Coastline ▶
25,760 km (16,000 miles)

Literacy rate
99% of Australians
can read and write

Major industries
Mining, industrial and
transport equipment, wine
production, food processing

Natural resources
Bauxite, coal, iron ore,
copper, tin

**Main crops and
livestock**
Wheat, barley,
sugar cane, fruits,
poultry, sheep

◀**Monetary unit**
Australian dollar

People to know

◄ Ned Kelly

Ned Kelly is a folk hero considered to be the father of Australian nationalism. He lived from 1855 to 1880. He was a bushworker who fought for the settlers' cause against British landowners and the police who protected their interests. Soon he became an outlaw. He was a good shot, and was famous for wearing an iron mask.

Russell Crowe ►

Russell Crowe is a world-famous actor who was born in New Zealand in 1964. He grew up in Australia. Crowe won the Oscar for Best Actor in 2001 for his performance in the film *Gladiator*.

◄ Cathy Freeman

Born in 1973, Cathy Freeman is a sprinter of Aborigine **descent**. She won the Olympic gold medal for 400 metres at the 2000 Olympic Games in Sydney. She has won over 30 international races, set nine home records and broken the world record in the 400-metre race. She proudly parades the Australian and Aborigine flags after winning a race.

More to read

Do you want to know more about Australia? Have a look at the books below.

Take your camera to Australia, Ted Park (Raintree, 2003) Your personal guidebook to Australia. Stunning photographs help you plan your trip and information on Australia's famous places, festivals and people show you why it is such an exciting place to visit.

Nations of the World: Australia, Robert Darlington (Raintree, 2003) Learn more about Australia – the cities, wilderness, economy and lifestyles of this fascinating country.

Continents: Australia and Oceania, M Fox (Heinemann Library, 2002) Learn about the continent's big cities, countryside and famous places. Find out about the major landforms, climate and vegetation, as well as the people and animals that live there.

Next Stop: Australia, Fred Martin (Heinemann Library, 1999) Go on a full tour of the country and learn about its past and present. Discover about the land, weather and animals and what life is really like for the people that live there.

Glossary

artesian basin low-lying area of land watered by many underground springs

billabong (BILL-uh-bong) shallow stream bed in Australia that is filled with water only during the rainy season

clan group of people who are all related

Commonwealth group of independent nations supported by the United Kingdom

continent one of the Earth's seven large land masses: Africa, Antarctica, Asia, Australia, Europe, North America and South America

convict person who has been sent to prison or to a penal colony for committing a crime

descent having ancestors from a particular group of people or family

equator imaginary line around the Earth, halfway between the North and South Poles

federation number of groups or states that are joined together under one government

fertile rich in nutrients and good for growing crops

immigrant person who has left their country to come to live in a new place

irrigate bring water to a place, through canals or pipes

mineral metal or other ore found in the ground

natural resource property of the land, such as water, minerals and trees, that occurs naturally and can be used by people

penal colony place where people who have committed crimes are sent to live together

prey animals that are hunted by other animals for food

refugee person who moves from their home country to seek safety in another country

sea level average level of the ocean's surface, used to measure the height of another place

species group of animals or plants whose members look and act alike and can breed with each other

suburb part of a city where people have their homes and there are not many big buildings or businesses

symbolic using symbols, which are images or movements that mean something everybody in a group recognizes

temperate climate with mild winters and cool summers, such as Australia or the UK

unique only one of its kind in the world

wharf dock or pier where ships are loaded and unloaded

Index